This Journal Belongs To......